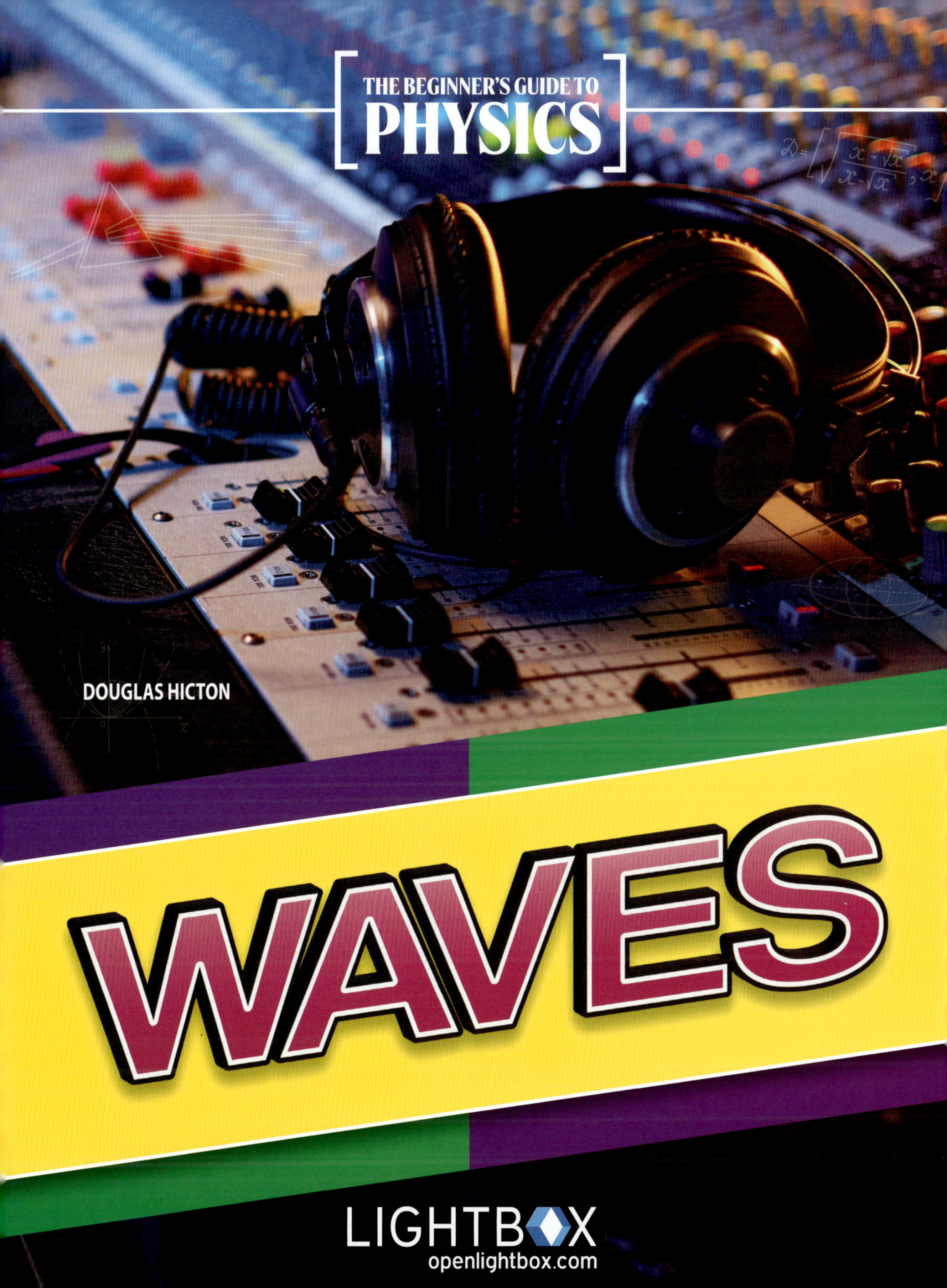
THE BEGINNER'S GUIDE TO
PHYSICS
DOUGLAS HICTON
WAVES
LIGHTBOX
openlightbox.com

Go to
www.openlightbox.com
and enter this book's
unique code.

ACCESS CODE

LBXK8282

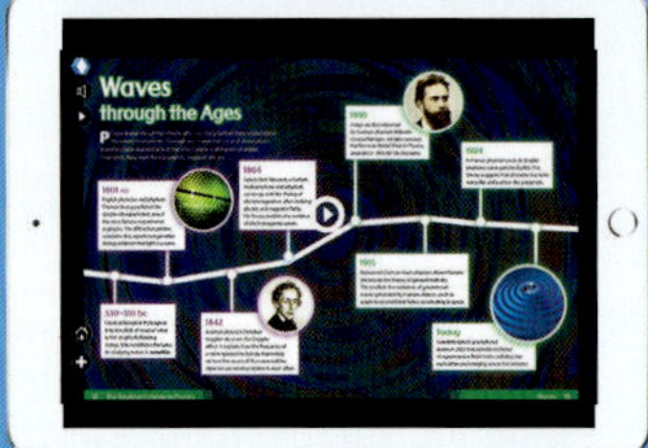

Lightbox is an all-inclusive digital solution for the teaching and learning of curriculum topics in an original, groundbreaking way. Lightbox is based on National Curriculum Standards.

LIGHTBOX SUPPLEMENTARY RESOURCES

SHARE
Share titles within your Learning Management System (LMS) or Library Circulation System

CURRICULUM
Find national and state curriculum correlations

CITATION
Create bibliographical references following APA, CMOS, and MLA styles

STANDARD FEATURES OF LIGHTBOX

AUDIO High-quality narration using text-to-speech system

ACTIVITIES Printable PDFs that can be emailed and graded

SLIDESHOWS Pictorial overviews of key concepts

VIDEOS Embedded high-definition video clips

WEBLINKS Curated links to external, child-safe resources

TRANSPARENCIES Step-by-step layering of maps, diagrams, charts, and timelines

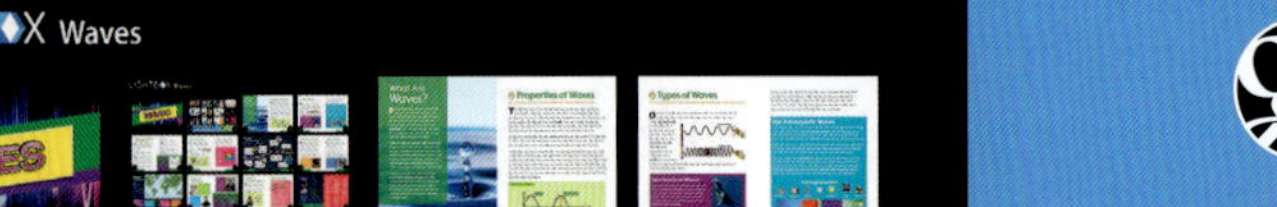

INTERACTIVE MAPS Interactive maps and aerial satellite imagery

QUIZZES Ten multiple-choice questions that are automatically graded and emailed for teacher assessment

KEY WORDS Matching key concepts to their definitions

This title is part of our Lightbox digital subscription

Lightbox Grades 6–8 Subscription
ISBN 978-1-5105-6068-0

Access hundreds of Lightbox titles with our digital subscription. Sign up for a **FREE** subscription trial at **www.openlightbox.com/trial**

The digital components of this book are guaranteed to stay active for at least five years from the date of publication.

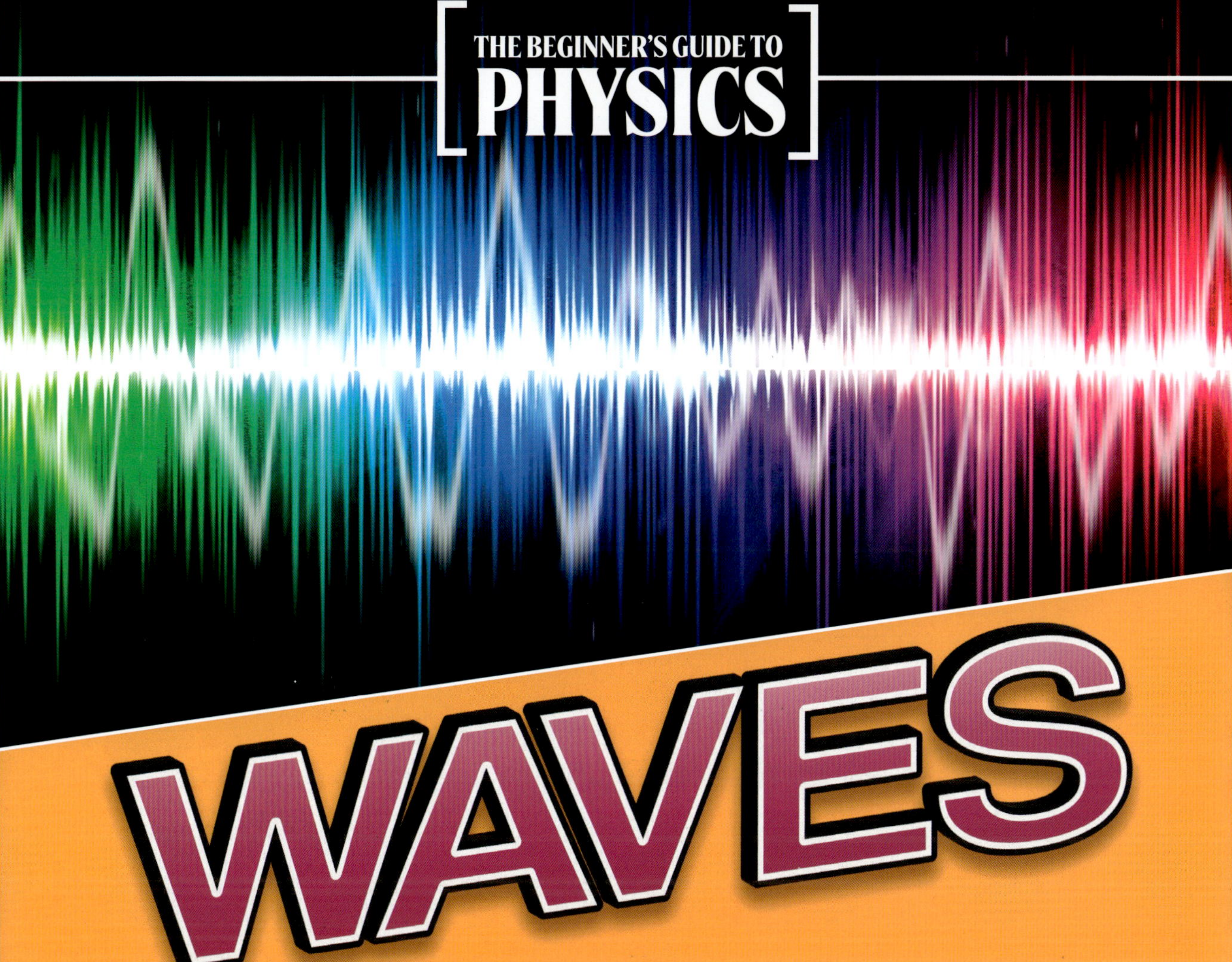

WAVES

Contents

What Are Waves?

Picture dropping a stone in a pond and seeing ripples spread out across the water. These ripples are examples of waves. All waves are disturbances that transfer energy. Waves travel through different **mediums**, such as solids, liquids, and gases. Some waves can even travel in the vacuum of space, where there is no matter.

Matter is made of particles called molecules. In gases, such as those in air, molecules are far apart. In liquids and solids, they are more closely packed together. When waves move through matter, their energy is passed along from molecule to molecule. However, the matter itself does not actually move forward.

Waves are everywhere, although some may be invisible. Sound waves make music. Light waves produce colors. Waves of water lap at beaches. Knowing how waves work is important to understanding how energy is transferred, or transmitted.

Properties of Waves

All waves share four basic properties. These are wavelength, amplitude, frequency, and period. A wavelength represents the length of a wave. It is the distance from one **crest** to the next crest or the distance from one **trough** to the next trough. Amplitude measures the distance of a wave from a crest or trough to the wave's resting position. Both wavelength and amplitude can be measured in units such as feet and meters, like any physical distance.

Frequency is the number of wave **cycles** that pass by in one second. It is measured in Hertz (Hz), with 1 Hz representing one cycle per second. The period indicates the time required for a wave to complete one cycle and is measured in seconds.

Visible light waves have relatively short wavelengths and high frequencies, while sound waves exhibit long wavelengths and low frequencies. Waves with higher frequencies carry more energy. This means that light travels much faster than sound. Light waves travel at a speed of about 186,000 miles (300,000 kilometers) per second. Sound waves only travel about 1,125 feet (343 meters) per second in air, explaining why people see lightning well before they hear the sound of thunder.

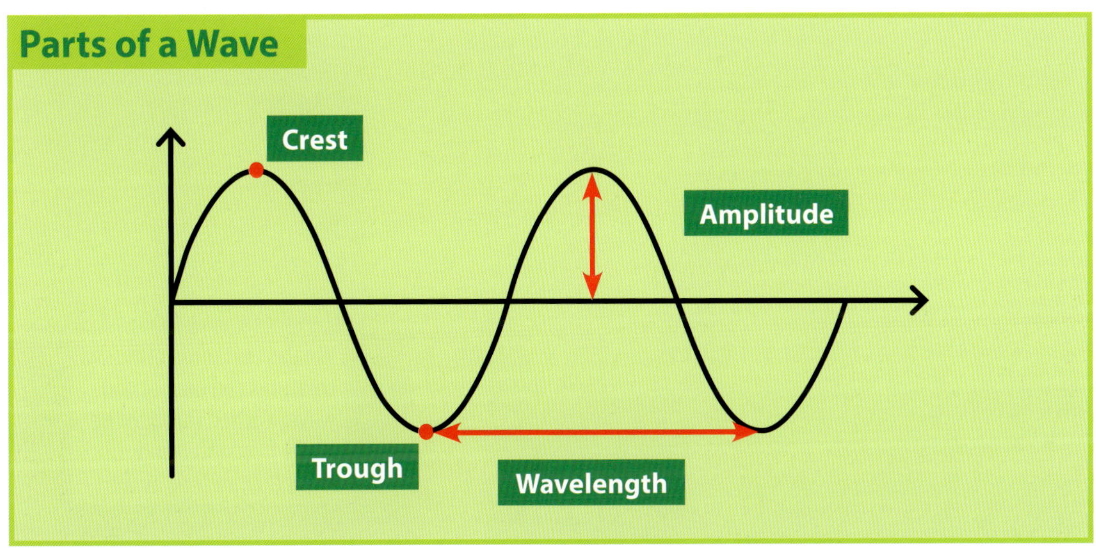

Types of Waves

One way to categorize waves is by the way they move. This movement is called **oscillation**. Transverse and longitudinal waves are the two basic types of waves. Transverse waves vibrate **perpendicular** to their direction of travel. They move up and down from their resting position. In longitudinal waves, oscillations occur **parallel** to the direction of travel. Some waves have both transverse and longitudinal components. They are called surface waves.

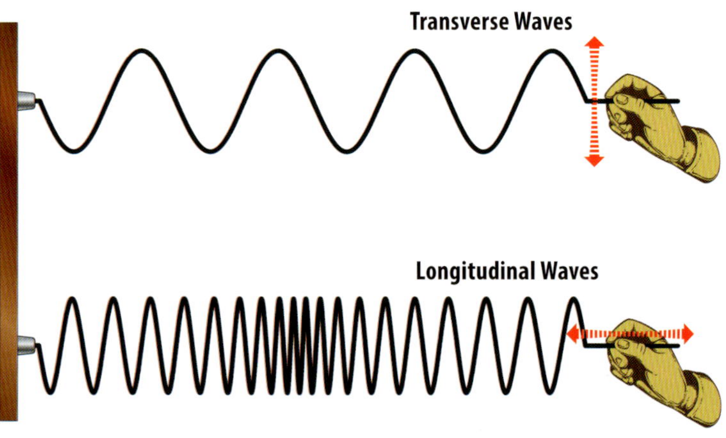

Mechanical Waves

Sound waves are mechanical, longitudinal waves that travel from a source through solids, liquids, and gases. Solids, such as steel, transmit sound best due to their densely packed particles. Water and other liquids also allow sound waves to travel long distances. Air and other gases are the least efficient for sound transmission.

Ripples in water and ocean waves are also mechanical waves. They transfer energy between water particles, creating visible wave motion. During earthquakes, seismic waves shake the ground and travel through Earth. These surface waves cause tremors and shake structures far from the **epicenter**.

Whales and some other sea creatures can hear sound waves carried through the water from thousands of miles (kilometers) away.

Waves can also be classified by how they travel. Mechanical waves need a medium to travel through. Solids, liquids, and gases can be used as mediums. Electromagnetic waves, on the other hand, can travel with or without a medium. Only electromagnetic waves, such as light, radio waves, and x-rays, are able to travel through the vacuum of space.

Electromagnetic Waves

Electromagnetic waves are transverse waves. They consist of electric and magnetic fields oscillating perpendicular to each other. The **electromagnetic spectrum** categorizes these waves by size. Radio waves have long wavelengths and are used to transmit radio and TV signals. Microwaves are used for cooking and communication. **Infrared** waves can be felt as heat and used in TV remotes.

Visible light only occupies a small part of the electromagnetic spectrum, but it makes sight possible. It is the part of the electromagnetic spectrum that lets people and animals see colors. Plants also need visible light. They use it for photosynthesis, the process by which they get energy.

Beyond visible light, there is **ultraviolet (UV)** light. Its main source is the Sun. The human body uses UV rays to produce Vitamin D, but too much exposure can also cause sunburns. X-rays, with their short wavelengths, pass through soft tissues and aid doctors in imaging and diagnostics. Gamma rays are the electromagnetic waves with the shortest wavelengths, highest frequencies, and most energy. They have applications in cancer treatment, industrial processes, and astrophysics.

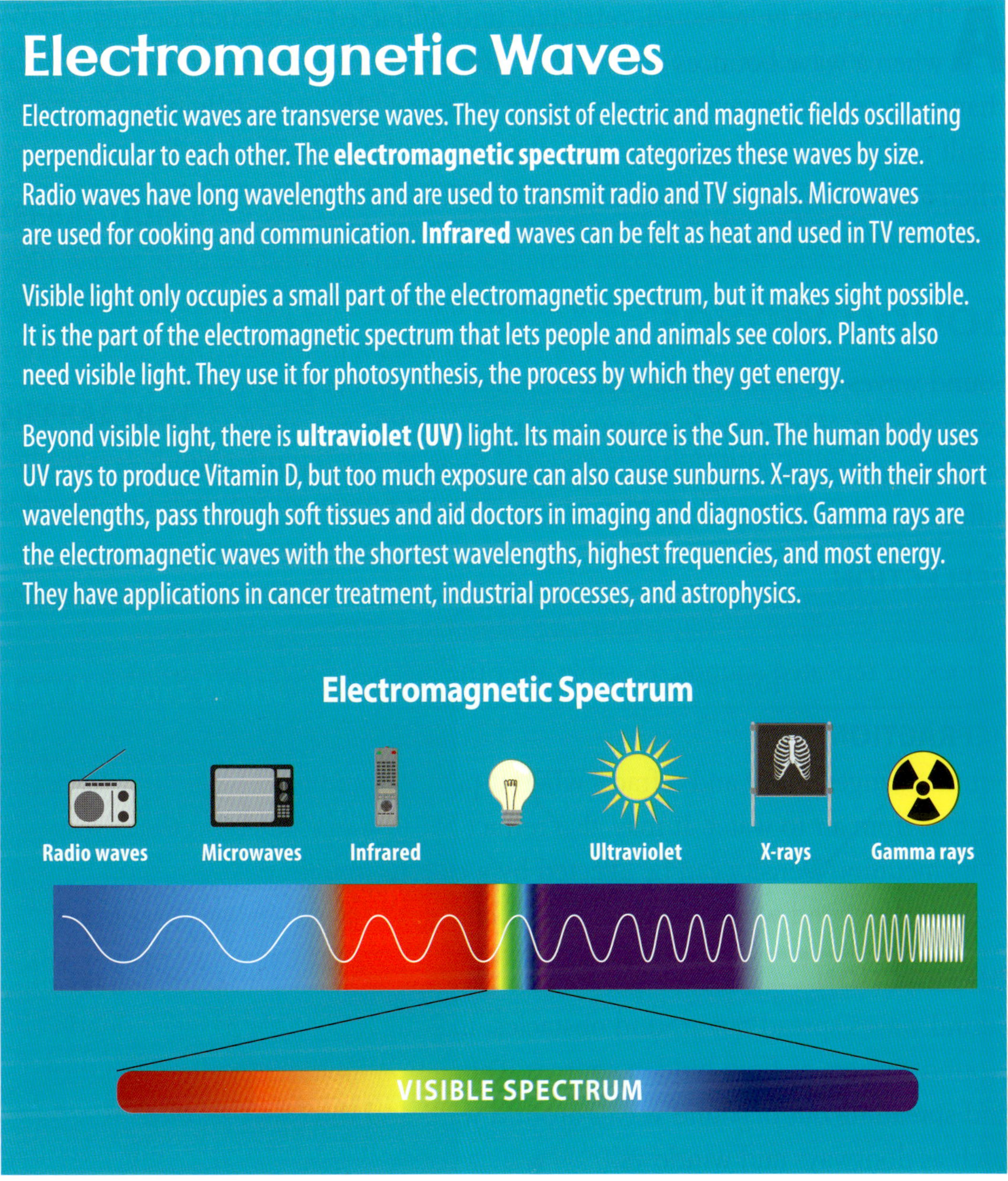

Waves through the Ages

People knew about the effects of waves long before they understood the waves themselves. Through experimentation and observation, scientists have learned about the structure and behavior of waves. Over time, they have found ways to measure waves.

1801 AD

English physician and physicist Thomas Young performs the double-slit experiment, one of the most famous experiments in physics. The diffraction pattern created in this experiment provides strong evidence that light is a wave.

1864

James Clerk Maxwell, a Scottish mathematician and physicist, comes up with the theory of electromagnetism after studying electric and magnetic fields. His theory predicts the existence of electromagnetic waves.

530–510 BC

Greek philosopher Pythagoras links the pitch of musical notes to the length of vibrating strings. This establishes the basis for studying waves in **acoustics**.

1842

Austrian physicist Christian Doppler discovers the Doppler effect. It explains how the frequency of a wave appears to change depending on how the observer and the source of the wave are moving relative to each other.

1895

X-rays are first observed by German physicist Wilhelm Conrad Röntgen. He later receives the first-ever Nobel Prize in Physics, awarded in 1901, for this discovery.

1924

In France, physicist Louis de Broglie proposes wave-particle duality. This theory suggests that all matter has both wave-like and particle-like properties.

1915

Renowned German-born physicist Albert Einstein introduces the theory of general relativity. This predicts the existence of gravitational waves generated by massive objects, such as supernovas and black holes, accelerating in space.

Today

Scientists detect gravitational waves in 2023 that provide evidence of supermassive black holes colliding into each other and merging throughout the universe.

Waves around the World

Waves of one kind or another are found everywhere on Earth. Water waves crash on coasts, lakeshores, and riverbanks around the world. Sound waves pass through nearly every molecule of matter on Earth, as do electromagnetic waves. Seismic waves have been detected beneath every ocean and on every continent.

1 Long-Distance Transmitter

Cutler, Maine, United States

The Very Low Frequency (VLF) Transmitter in Cutler is one of the most powerful radio transmitters in the world. It uses radio waves to communicate with U.S. Navy submarines underwater and can transmit signals thousands of miles (kilometers) away.

2 Ancient Acoustics

Epidavros, Greece

The Theater of Epidaurus, built 2,400 years ago by the ancient Greeks, is known for its extraordinary acoustics. Centuries ago, people claimed that spectators in the back row of the 12,000-seat theater could hear normally spoken dialogue clearly.

3 Ionosphere Research

Vasilsursk, Russia

The Sura Ionospheric Heating Facility was built in 1981 as a research laboratory to study the ionosphere. This is the upper layer of Earth's atmosphere. The ionosphere reflects radio waves and plays an important role in long-distance radio communications.

4 Largest Coral Reef System

Pacific Ocean, near Queensland, Australia

Visible from space, the 1,430-mile (2,300-km) Great Barrier Reef is the world's largest living structure. It creates a natural barrier that absorbs and refracts ocean waves, protecting nearby coastal areas from storms and floods.

Quiz

1 What is the unit of measurement for the frequency of a wave?

2 Who first used wireless radio for communication?

3 In what direction do transverse waves vibrate?

4 Which waves travel can travel through the vacuum of space?

5 Which color has the longest wavelength?

6 What are the two main types of seismic body waves?

7 Who first observed x-rays?

8 What are four basic properties common to all waves?

9 In what unit is the loudness or softness of a sound measured?

10 Which scientist used a prism to split sunlight into different colors in 1666?

ANSWERS

1. Hertz (Hz) 2. Guglielmo Marconi 3. Perpendicular to their direction of travel 4. Electromagnetic waves 5. Red 6. Primary waves (P-waves) and secondary waves (S-waves) 7. Wilhelm Conrad Röntgen 8. Wavelength, amplitude, frequency, and period 9. Decibels (dB) 10. Isaac Newton

Key Words

acoustics: the branch of physics that studies the properties of sound

crest: the highest point, or peak, of a wave

cycles: individual wavelengths, or full completions of a wave

diffusing: spreading out evenly

electromagnetic spectrum: the range organizing electromagnetic waves from largest to smallest

epicenter: the central point on Earth's surface directly above the origin of an earthquake

infrared: a range of invisible electromagnetic waves with longer wavelengths and lower frequencies than red light

mediums: substances that make the transfer of energy from one point to another possible

meteorology: the branch of science that studies and forecasts the weather

nanometers: 1 billionth of individual meters (0.000000001 m)

oscillation: movement back and forth at a regular speed

parallel: in the same direction forward or backward

pendulum: a weight that hangs from a fixed point and can freely swing forward or backward

perpendicular: at a right angle, or an angle of 90°

prism: a glass or other transparent object, often triangular, with refracting surfaces at angles less than 90°

trough: the lowest point of a wave

ultraviolet (UV): a range of invisible electromagnetic waves with shorter wavelengths and higher frequencies than violet light

velocity: speed in a given direction

Index

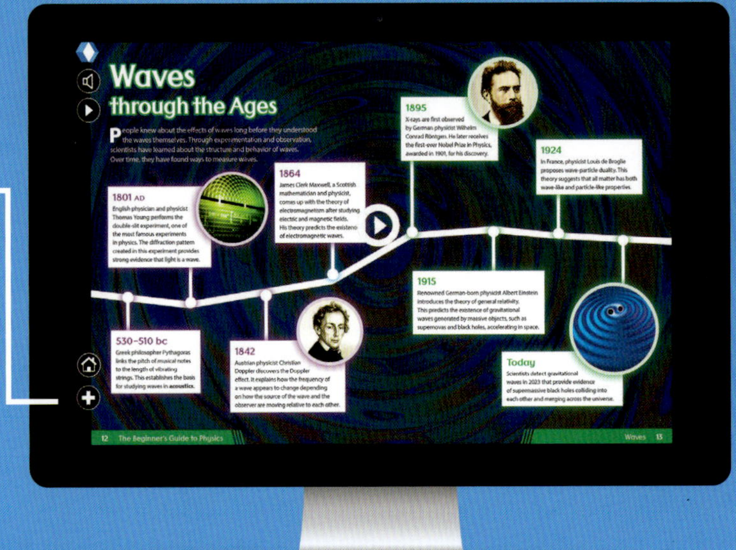

SUPPLEMENTARY RESOURCES

Click on the plus icon found in the bottom left corner of each spread to open additional teacher resources.

- Download and print the book's quizzes and activities
- Access curriculum correlations
- Explore additional web applications that enhance the Lightbox experience

LIGHTBOX DIGITAL TITLES
Packed full of integrated media

VIDEOS

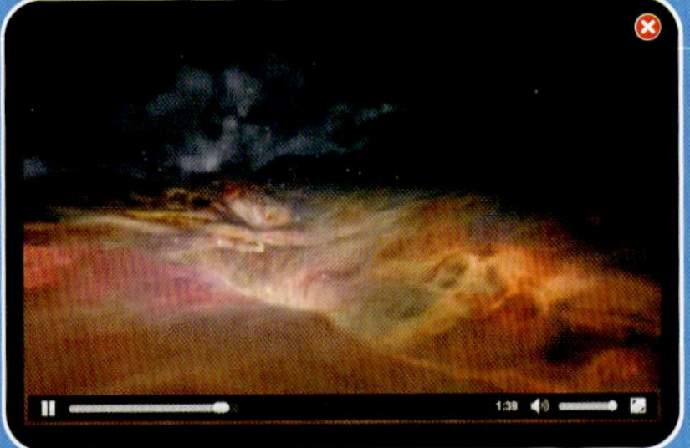

INTERACTIVE MAPS

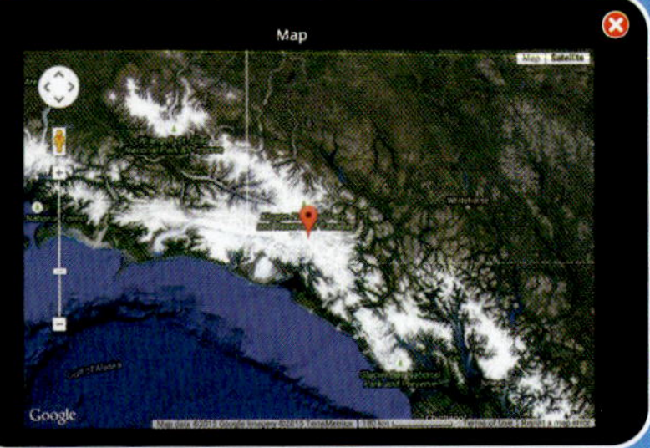

WEBLINKS

SLIDESHOWS

QUIZZES

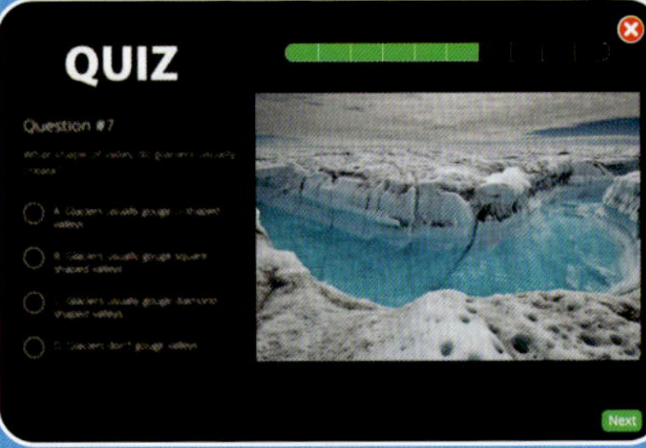

OPTIMIZED FOR

- ✓ TABLETS
- ✓ SMART BOARDS
- ✓ COMPUTERS
- ✓ AND MUCH MORE!

Published by Lightbox Learning Inc.
276 5th Avenue, Suite 704 #917
New York, NY 10001
Website: www.openlightbox.com

Library of Congress Control Number: 2024936117

ISBN 978-1-5105-6707-8 (hardcover)
ISBN 978-1-5105-6708-5 (multi-user static eBook)
ISBN 978-1-5105-8087-9 (multi-user interactive eBook)

Printed in Guangzhou, China
1 2 3 4 5 6 7 8 9 0 28 27 26 25 24

062024
111023

Project Coordinator Priyanka Das
Designer Mandy Christiansen
Layout Jean Faye Rodriguez

Photo Credits
Every reasonable effort has been made to trace ownership and to obtain permission to reprint copyright material. The publisher would be pleased to have any errors or omissions brought to its attention so that they may be corrected in subsequent printings.

The publisher acknowledges Getty Images and Shutterstock as its primary image suppliers for this title.